THE QUEEN'S VISIT TO CHINA & HONG KONG

女王訪問中國及香港

Text: John Osman
Photographs: Tim Graham

PITKIN PICTORIALS

The Queen's Visit to China and Hong Kong

The first European to gain any real knowledge of China was Marco Polo. He travelled there in 1271 on an embassy for the Pope. He became a legend after spending 17 years in the lands of the Grand Khan of Tartary. But, in the 20th century, it does not take as long to create a legend: and that is what The Queen's one-week visit to China has already become. With instant air travel, live television and radio, and massive newspaper publicity, the world-wide impact of the monarch's 3000-mile odyssey around such a diverse and enormous country was immediate. As just one of many journalists privileged to join The Queen on her travels, I found the experience breathtakingly exciting; and it seems appropriate that the royal journey has started a rush to China by British tourists. As the director of the China National Tourist Office in London put it, 'The Queen has opened the eyes of Westerners, who believed China was a closed and secretive place.'

The Chinese themselves decided from the word 'Go' to treat Elizabeth II as, what one Peking official called, 'the Queen of Queens'. And though she is the most-travelled sovereign of all time, there is no doubt that Her Majesty was absorbed and impressed by China from the moment she arrived.

The Queen's itinerary was: Peking, Shanghai, Xian, Kunming, Canton and, after the visit to mainland China, Hong Kong.

Day 1: Sunday 12 October

The royal progress began in the capital of China, when The Queen flew into the airport at Peking, in a British Airways Tristar, on a sunny autumn afternoon. It was a genuinely historic moment—the first British monarch ever to set foot in China, the 'Middle Kingdom', the home of a quarter of the world's population—more than one billion Chinese people. Moreover, as a result of the 1984 agreement between Britain and China by which Hong Kong will revert to Chinese sovereignty in 1997, The Queen is the first British monarch since George II to have no claim to any part of China. Given the significance of the occasion, the arrival ceremony was, although polite and smiling, notably low-key.

THIS PAGE: (Above) *The Royal Party visiting another part of the Forbidden City, the Halls of Harmony.*

THIS PAGE: (Left) *More sight-seeing in Peking for The Queen and Prince Philip: visiting the spectacular Temple of Heaven, which was constructed originally in the 15th century but has since been substantially rebuilt.*

FACING PAGE: (Above) *Before her walk along the Wall, The Queen had talks with 82-year-old Chairman Deng Xiaoping, the 'strong-man' behind China's modernisation programme and a prominent figure from China's turbulent political past.*

FACING PAGE: (Below) *The Queen and Prince Philip's 'walk of a lifetime' took them along the Badaling section of the Great Wall of China. Reputedly the only man-made object visible on earth from outer space, the Great Wall dates back over 2000 years. Although The Queen trod the carefully hewn stones of the Ming era, parts of the original wall are now little more than a line of crumbling mud bricks reaching out across distant deserts.*

After the 16-hour flight from London, and a re-fuelling stop in Muscat, the Tristar taxied to a halt with the Royal Standard flying above the cockpit. The first to greet The Queen on board were The Duke of Edinburgh (who had arrived from Tokyo half an hour beforehand), and the urbane British Ambassador in Peking, Sir Richard Evans. Minutes later, The Queen, wearing a yellow and black silk linen outfit with a wide-brimmed white hat, emerged into the sunshine to be greeted by the Chinese welcoming party which included no fewer than four government ministers, led by the Foreign Minister, Wu Xueqian. On the British side, the Minister in attendance on The Queen was the Foreign Secretary, Sir Geoffrey Howe. After receiving bouquets from two small children, The Queen was driven ten miles to a new and lavish State guest house, Number 18, Diaoyutai—which means 'Angler's Terrace.' It takes its name from a 12th-century imperial official who lived in seclusion there disguised as a fisherman. The area became an imperial pleasure park but fell later into neglect and decay, until, in 1958, the place was rebuilt around the ruins of the ancient terrace and set in a wooded park complete with lakes, water-falls, hills and rockeries—all artificial—plus a fine collection of rare and exotic plants.

Other crowned Heads of State have preceded The Queen to China—for instance, King Juan Carlos of Spain and Queen Margarethe of Denmark. However, this visit by the British Monarch has far greater significance for the Chinese, largely because of the legacies of imperial history. When Lord McCartney led the first British mission to China in 1793 he refused to kowtow to the Emperor and the relationship between the two countries for the following centuries has often been painful and stormy. All this now lies in the past and a mutual understanding has developed, culminating in The Queen's first steps on Chinese soil.

Day 2: Monday 13 October

This was the real beginning of the royal tour, conspicuously televisual, highly publicised, full of colour. The Queen and Prince Philip were welcomed at a ceremony staged in front of the Great Hall of the People in Tiananmen Square—Tiananmen, the 'Gate of Heavenly Peace', being the traditional site for the proclamation of Chinese imperial edicts and the place from which Mao Zedong announced the establishment in October 1949 of the

ABOVE: *Arriving at Shanghai airport on the fourth day of their tour, The Queen and Prince Philip are greeted enthusiastically by local children, dressed in miniature paper horses and welcoming the Royal couple with a dancing display.*

LEFT: *The Queen being presented with gifts at the Xi Jiao Guest House in Shanghai, where she resided on 15 October.*

People's Republic of China. The vast 98-acre square has witnessed turbulent episodes; it was here that Red Guards were marshalled during the Cultural Revolution in the 1960s; and here, that crowds gathered to mourn the death of Zhou Enlai and to demonstrate their defiance of, and distaste for, the notorious 'Gang of Four'. The Queen's arrival, though, was a happy occasion; a gasp of pleasure went up from the Chinese when The Queen stepped out of her limousine wearing, appropriately, a red coat and hat. Twenty-one guns fired a salute; bands played the Chinese and British National Anthems; The Queen inspected a Guard of Honour of the Chinese Armed Forces; and Chinese children sang and danced in warm welcome.

After the welcoming ceremony came The Queen's first formal talks in China with a Chinese leader. In the Great Hall of the People she sat down with President Li Xiannian, aged 77. Born into a peasant family, President Li is China's first Head of State since the

Cultural Revolution, the post having been abolished in the 1970s and re-established in 1983. A member of the all-powerful standing committee of the ruling Politburo of the Chinese Communist Party, President Li has survived several mass movements over the past 30 years which brought down other senior Chinese leaders, and was a distinguished soldier and guerilla leader in the 1940s, as well as a prominent 'Long Marcher'. He did most of the talking at this first encounter with The Queen. After the talks, The Queen

*   *   *

ABOVE: *The Queen peering down on the serried ranks of terracotta soldiers, modelled over 2000 years ago to guard the tomb of Emperor Qin Shihuang and unearthed at Lingtong, Xian in 1975. The 7000 life-size warriors are divided into three main groups, two fighting units and one command unit. They now stand within a huge hangar-like building which protects them (and archaeologists still excavating the site) from the weather.*

returned to her guest house to entertain 160 British, Commonwealth and Chinese journalists and cameramen at a Press Reception. This has become traditional on all the royal tours I have covered, with The Queen making a point of saying 'Hello' to writers and photographers travelling with her. As is customary, she was a charming hostess, knowledgeable about our work and our problems, ready with sympathetic comments and interested questions.

In the afternoon, The Queen came face-to-face with ordinary Chinese people for the first time when she visited the 'Forbidden City' of the Ming and Qing dynasty emperors. She walked from the Gate of Supreme Harmony, through a maze of courtyards, temples and pavilions, to the Gate of Heavenly Purity. Crowds rushed across the cobble-stones and pathways trying to catch a glimpse of her; and Chinese security officers had their work cut out in controlling the masses. The Queen had specifically

THIS PAGE: (Above) *The Queen and Prince Philip arriving in Kunming, 'the City of Eternal Spring', to be greeted by the Governor of Yunnan and more happy children, singing, dancing and gaily dressed in colourful costumes. The new BAe 146 of The Queen's Flight was used for internal flights during the tour. (Left) The Queen (wearing an emerald green and black spotted dress under an emerald green coat) is being presented with gifts at the Kunming Institute of Nationalities, which caters for the numerous ethnic minorities in Yunnan province.*

FACING PAGE: *Saffron-robed Buddhist monks conducting the fascinated Royal couple round Huating Temple, in the Western Hills. Five-hundred-odd sculpted faces peer down from the surrounding walls, and sounding gongs, burning incense and great statues of Buddha create a unique atmosphere in this place of worship.*

asked that no attempt should be made to seal off the sights from ordinary tourists while she was there, in accordance with her wish to see, and be seen by, the people wherever she goes. The 'Forbidden City' attracts millions of visitors every year, being the administrative centre of the old Chinese empire as well as the residence of the imperial household. Originally 9999 buildings stood within the moat and 35-foot walls; and the last Emperor, Puyi, remained resident in the private quarters until 1924. The following year the 250-acre complex was renamed the Palace Museum and it is now designated a national treasure.

The last event of the day was the State Banquet, one of the most exotic and extraordinary meals I have ever eaten (and enjoyed) in my life. The Queen seemed to like it, too, employing chopsticks with confidence and skill. The 10-course banquet included such delicacies as sea-slug, shark's fin, and a small fruit known as dragon's eyes. The Queen was marvellously regal in a heavy pink silk crêpe dress decorated with clusters of peony, the Chinese national flower. She wore a tiara, with a necklace and ear-rings of diamonds and rubies, and was seated between President Li and the Chinese Premier, Zhao Ziyang—the presence of both dignitaries being regarded as a signal honour. The table decorations were fantastic: live fish swam in a pot under bridges of water melon in front of The Queen, while on the central table stood two large illuminated model peacocks.

The speeches of President Li and The Queen both emphasised the new closeness of Sino-British relations. President Li described The Queen's visit as 'an important milestone' and said: 'The satisfactory settlement by the two governments in 1984 of the Hong Kong question, which was left over from the past, ushered in a new historical period in our bilateral relations. It also set a good example of settling disputes between States through peaceful negotiations.'

Replying, The Queen said that links between the two countries were today closer than they had ever been. That owed much to the Hong Kong settlement. 'Both our countries,' she remarked, 'are committed to doing everything possible to maintain Hong Kong's continued stability and prosperity.' She announced the setting-up of the Royal Society's 'Royal Fellowships for China', under which China would send some of its best scientists to Britain to work with British scientists. These fellowships, she said, would

cover the most challenging areas of research, and it was hoped that links would be forged not only between China and Britain, but with Britain's partners in Europe, the Commonwealth, and the English-speaking world.

Day 3: Tuesday 14 October

This was probably the single most important day of the whole tour. First, the Communist Party General Secretary, Hu Yaobang, conducted The Queen and Prince Philip on a tour of the Chinese leaders' residential area, Zhongnanhai, once part of the palace complex and now the headquarters of the Chinese Communist Party. Then— the Summit itself: the royal encounter with China's strong man, the driving force behind China's modernisation programme, 82-year-old Deng Xiaoping.

Born in Sichuan, Deng took part in the Long March in 1934, and has survived a turbulent political career to attain his present eminence as leader of one-quarter of the world's population. He was the second-highest ranking victim of the Cultural Revolution, being relieved of his posts as General Secretary of the Communist Party, member of the ruling Politburo, and Vice-Premier, when he was purged in 1966. In 1973 he was rehabilitated and made a party Vice-Chairman; by 1975 he was once again in the Politburo— then, in 1976, his second downfall was brought about by leftists. After their expulsion, following the death of Mao Zedong, Deng regained in 1977 the posts he had lost the previous year.

'Thank you for meeting such an old man as me,' was his opening remark to The Queen as he greeted her. She told him that he was younger than her own mother, Queen Elizabeth The Queen Mother, who is 86. Deng often jokes that the reason he has lived so long is that he smokes a lot—but he politely refrained from smoking throughout his conversation with The Queen in his personal villa, and for most of the private luncheon he gave for her in a Ming dynasty pavilion. Eventually, The Queen turned to him and remarked that she was sure he would like a smoke; and he gratefully and smilingly agreed.

After a visit to a kindergarten for children of parents who are both working, The Queen went sight-seeing again: this time, to the Great Wall of China, and to the Ming Tombs. At the age of 60, she tackled the Wall with determination, walking and climbing up a 45-degree incline, going further

Continued on page 14

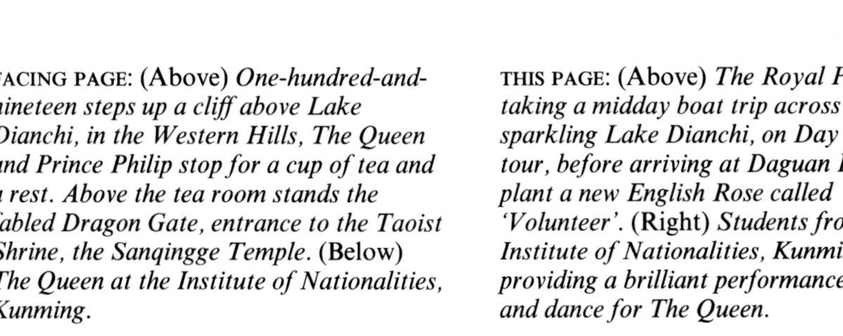

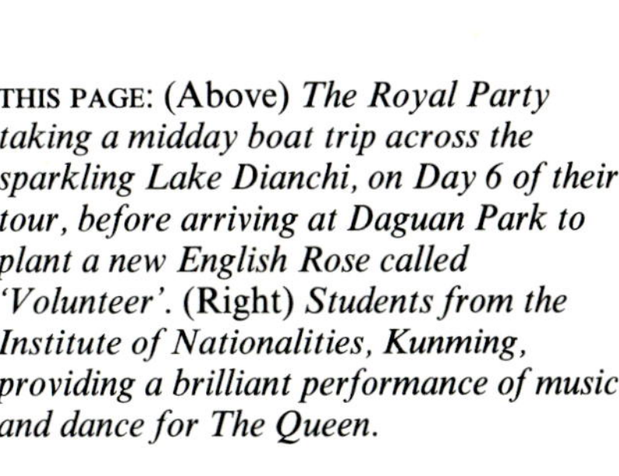

FACING PAGE: (Above) *One-hundred-and-nineteen steps up a cliff above Lake Dianchi, in the Western Hills, The Queen and Prince Philip stop for a cup of tea and a rest. Above the tea room stands the fabled Dragon Gate, entrance to the Taoist Shrine, the Sanqingge Temple. (Below) The Queen at the Institute of Nationalities, Kunming.*

THIS PAGE: (Above) *The Royal Party taking a midday boat trip across the sparkling Lake Dianchi, on Day 6 of their tour, before arriving at Daguan Park to plant a new English Rose called 'Volunteer'. (Right) Students from the Institute of Nationalities, Kunming, providing a brilliant performance of music and dance for The Queen.*

11

The State Banquet at Peking

The State Banquet at Peking, on Monday 13 October, was one of the most brilliant and important functions of The Queen's visit to China. On these pages are scenes from the glittering occasion.

In the picture above, The Queen, resplendent in tiara and shimmering dress, is with her hosts, President Li and his wife Madame Lin Jiamei, in Peking's Great Hall of the People. The tables were laid with fantastic decorations, such as the two shown on the left, carved from fruit and vegetables in the shape of birds and flowers.

Replying to President Li's address, The Queen (top of facing page) praised the Hong Kong settlement signed by China and Great Britain in 1984 and said that links between the two countries were closer today than they had ever been. Below this picture, we see The Queen and President Li exchanging toasts. The Queen was then instructed in the tricky skill of using chopsticks, before commencing the 10-course feast of beautifully presented dishes. Afterwards, The Queen met some of the performers (bottom left of facing page) who provided the colourful banquet entertainment.

The Queen's pink silk crêpe dress, worn with a necklace and earrings of diamonds and rubies, was encrusted with lavish beading and embroidered with clusters of peony, the Chinese national flower. It was specially designed by Ian Thomas for the Chinese visit.

than either President Reagan or ex-President Nixon when they visited the same place. Wearing sensible rubber-soled shoes, she posed for pictures, and took her own photographs.

The Great Wall, as it is known today, first took shape in about 200 BC when China's first unifier linked up other defensive walls to form a defence barrier; but the fabric of the present wall dates mainly from the Ming dynasty. It was one of the first projects undertaken following the expulsion of the Mongols, and building lasted for over 100 years from AD 1368 to 1500. It stretched for 2484 miles when completed. The section at Badaling seen by The Queen is a fine example of Ming military architecture protecting one of the main passes from the north into Peking. The Wall is 7.8 metres high, wide enough for ten soldiers to march along or five horsemen riding abreast.

When The Queen started the tricky descent from the Wall, she called out: 'It's much worse going down than coming up!' She held an iron rail but needed no help down. Turning to her private secretary, Sir William Heseltine, she added, with a grin, 'I don't think Bill Heseltine will be the same again.' He nodded in apparent agreement.

The last official function of this momentous day was a farewell call on The Queen by Premier Zhao Ziyang. On the following morning the Royal Party flew to Shanghai.

Day 4: Wednesday 15 October

The people of Shanghai, China's largest and most teeming metropolis, turned out in their millions to provide a reception in startling contrast to the formality of Peking. Gone are the days when missionaries once declared that, if God let Shanghai endure, he owed an apology to Sodom and Gomorrah; yet, there is a lingering cosmopolitanism and sophistication about the city—an old bridge-head of imperialism and commerce, which is irresistibly stimulating. Cheering, clapping, exploding firecrackers, the citizens of Shanghai not only swarmed about The Queen when she went for an amazing walkabout in the heart of this human ant-hill, but they packed the famous Bund

*　　*　　*

LEFT: *Her Majesty The Queen, dressed in a red crêpe evening dress, attending a dinner hosted by the head of Yunnan Provincial Government. A cultural performance followed the feast, completing Day 6 of the royal tour.*

and waterfront till late at night, trying to watch the Royal Marines Band Beat the Retreat on the quayside. In her walk-about, The Queen strolled just a few feet from seething masses of people, with her entourage. She paused in the attractive 'Teahouse of the Heart of the Lake', which is approached by a zigzag bridge designed to keep away evil spirits—they can travel only in straight lines! The teahouse was built two centuries ago on a goldfish pond.

In place of the usual teahouse customers' uproar, a flautist from the Shanghai Conservatoire played tunes such as 'In an English Country Garden' while The Queen took two cups of green Dragon Well tea. Other special musical effects in Shanghai included tinkering about with the chimes of a public clock so that, instead of playing 'The East is Red', the sound of 'Big Ben' rang out. And, at a luncheon for The Queen in Shanghai, yet more British melodies were played on Chinese instruments. Despite the unfamiliarity of their sound, I managed to recognise a Scottish reel, 'Greensleeves', 'No Place like Home', and, inevitably, 'Auld Lang Syne'. After luncheon, The Queen went into a shop to look at some carpets and was asked if she was planning to buy. 'Not now,' she answered, 'but perhaps later'. Her private secretary was then asked if she would pay by American Express, and he shook his head and joked: 'I would have thought that the credit was good enough, wouldn't you?'

While the royal programme went ahead, elsewhere in Shanghai 15 British firms were signing 14 agreements with Chinese organisations worth hundreds of millions of pounds. I went along to the signing ceremony in the Peace Hotel, which once upon a time was the Cathay Hotel, owned by the Sassoon family, and the place where Noel Coward wrote 'Private Lives'. The President of the Sino-British Trade Council, Sir Eric Sharp, who is also the head of Cable and Wireless, told me that the potential existed for contracts worth billions of pounds; and it is hoped that The Queen's visit will give a major boost to bi-lateral trade. The Shanghai programme ended with The Queen giving a return banquet on board *Britannia*. It was a memorable day.

* * *

RIGHT: (Above) *Red carpets and carnations for The Queen, dressed in blue and white silk for her visit to Canton. Her bouquet is presented by the grandson of a local governor.* (Below) *Sharing her walkabout with crowds of excited children.*

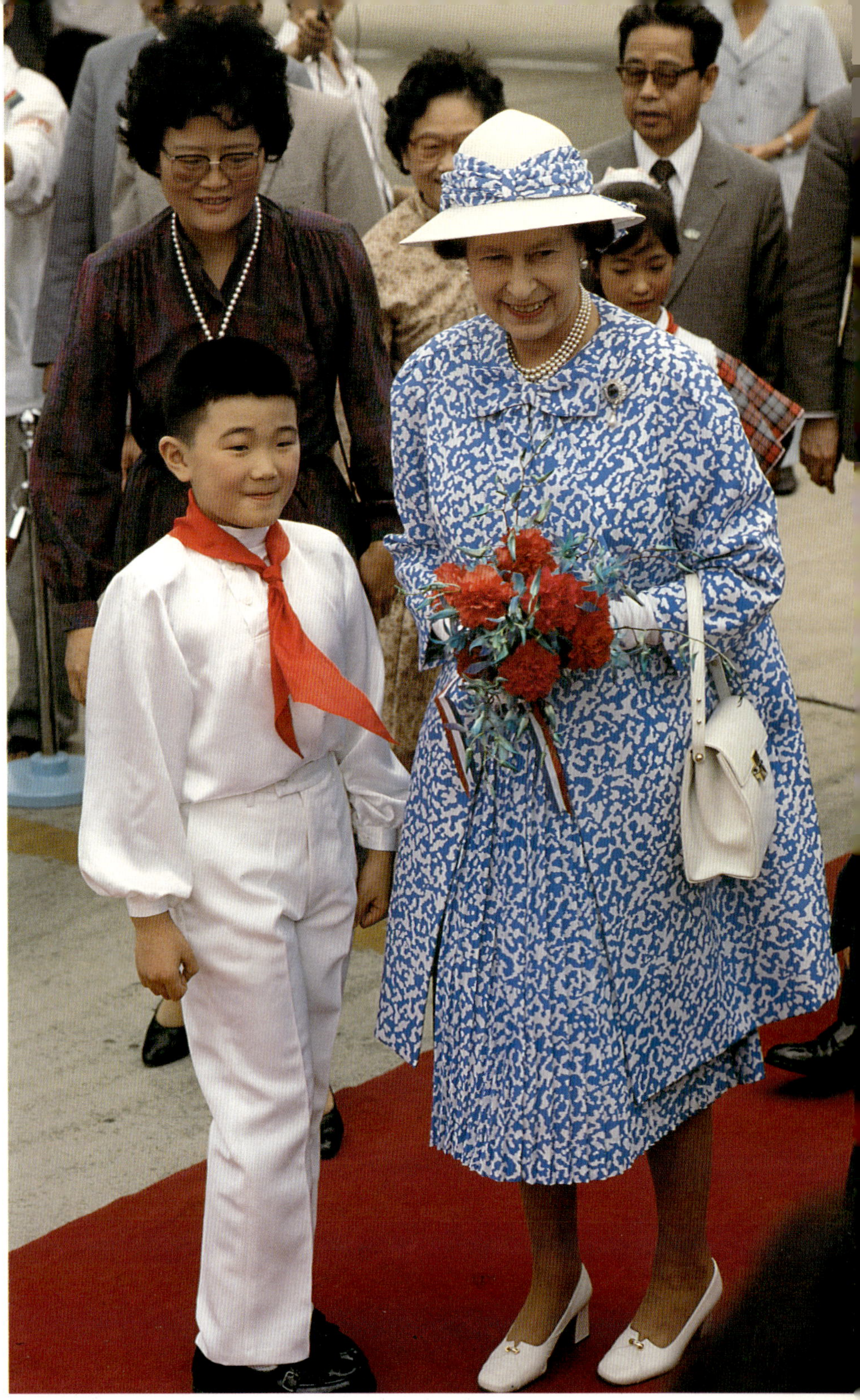

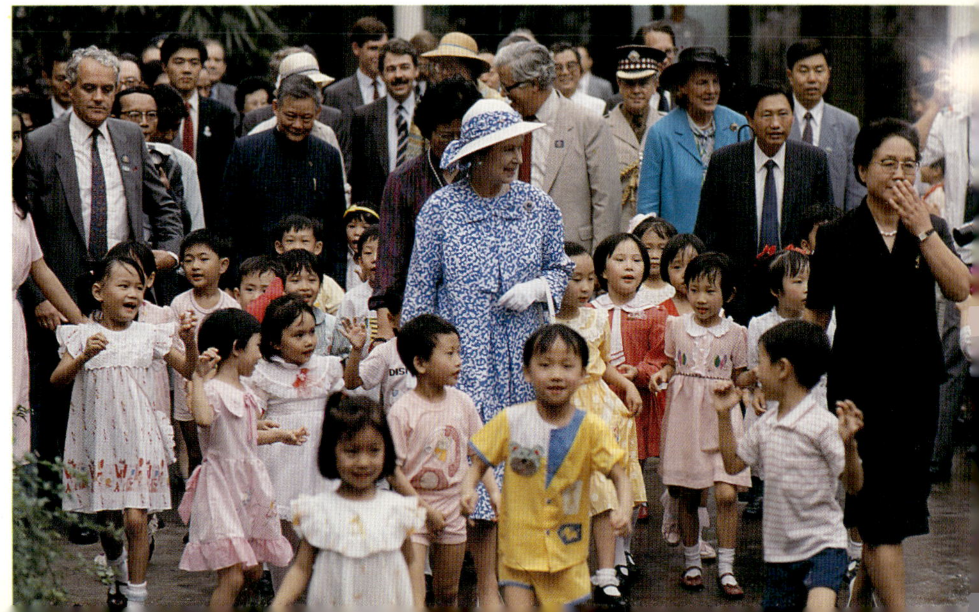

Day 5: Thursday 16 October

From Shanghai, on the coast of South China, The Queen flew inland to the dusty heart of central China—to Xian. For the first time on her journeying in China, she travelled in a BAe 146 of The Queen's Flight, instead of the Tristar. Xian was once the capital of China and of the State of Qin, under which China was first unified. The emperor who achieved that unification was the first Qin emperor, Qin Shi-huang, who died in 209 BC... and it was because of that ancient ruler that The Queen found herself in Xian. For there, just 12 years ago, peasants digging a well found a hidden army of life-size terracotta figures some 7000 strong. They had been undiscovered for over 2000 years, guarding the tomb of Qin Shihuang. Probably the most spectacular archaeological find of the century, the extraordinary army consists of three main groups of warriors, two fighting units and one command unit, all drawn up in battle formation. The Queen, who in her time has reviewed many Guards of Honour, had never before inspected one like this, and is unlikely ever to do so again. First, she gazed down on their serried ranks; then she walked down into the excavated vault to take a close look at

the warriors, gently touching some of the tall statues. The Queen looked up into their faces, every one different, and modelled perhaps on an individual actually in the Emperor's Guards. She studied the fine detail of the uniforms, then walked round the top of the excavation to watch Chinese archaeologists, concentrating on their work and apparently oblivious to her presence. But hundreds of other Chinese crowded curiously round the museum site, with a few Chinese children managing to evade security men and open the windows of the vast, hangar-like building which protects the warriors. The children pointed excitedly at The Queen—until they were briskly moved away. After viewing the vault, The Queen studied a large bronze chariot removed from a pit some 65 feet from the tomb of the emperor, which has not itself yet been excavated. The survival

of the buried treasures over two millennia is remarkable—especially since Qin Shihuang inspired such fear and hatred that, when the dynasty was overthrown not long after his death, his capital was systematically destroyed.

These days, Xian is the capital of Shaanxi province with about two and a half million inhabitants, thousands of whom greeted The Queen on her arrival there. Xian is 'twinned' with the city of Edinburgh, and 18 students from Edinburgh University, of which Prince Philip is the Chancellor, are studying Chinese at the North-Western University of Xian.

From Xian, The Queen and Prince Philip flew on to Kunming, in southeast China, not far from the borders of Vietnam and Burma. Known as 'the City of Eternal Spring' because of a mild climate resulting from its altitude of over 5000 feet, Kunming is the capital of Yunnan province, a border region with a large population of non-Chinese ethnic minorities. Representatives of those minority nationalities offered The Queen a traditional welcome when she was greeted at the airport by the Governor of Yunnan, He Zhixiang. Hundreds of thousands of the one and a half million inhabitants of Kunming crowded the streets of the city (somewhat off the tourist track) to see The Queen; and thousands more waited outside her guest house late into the night to try and get a glimpse of her. Built in the 1930s for the old Kuomintang Commander of Yunnan, the Xiyuan guest house, as it is known, is a French-style villa set in a walled garden, on the western shore of Lake Dianchi with the Western Hills behind.

Day 6: Friday 17 October

This was one of the most pleasant and colourful days of the entire tour, full of contrast. The Queen drove into the Western Hills overlooking Kunming and Lake Dianchi, the sixth largest freshwater lake in China, with a perimeter (according to an ancient poem) of 500 miles. There are magnificent views over the lake, the most spectacular of which is from the Dragon Gate, reached by steps cut in a sheer cliff, all laboriously carved by Taoist monks over a period of 72 years from 1781 to 1855. The Queen's first visit was to the Sanqingge Temple, originally built as a country villa for a prince of Liang in the Mongol period; then later used as a temple dedicated to three of the main deities in Taoism. Then, leaving the Taoists, The Queen and Prince Philip went on to visit the Buddhists; from Sanqingge Temple to Huating Temple. It is still a place of worship, so saffron-robed monks conducted the royal couple round their temple, with gongs sounding, incense burning, and great statues of Buddha alongside hundreds of strange carvings staring down upon the entourage.

Continued on page 21

★   ★   ★

THIS PAGE: (Above) *The Queen drinks a toast.* (Centre and below) *As spectators and performers, the Cantonese children share their enjoyment with The Queen—a happy onlooker of activities at the Children's Palace.*

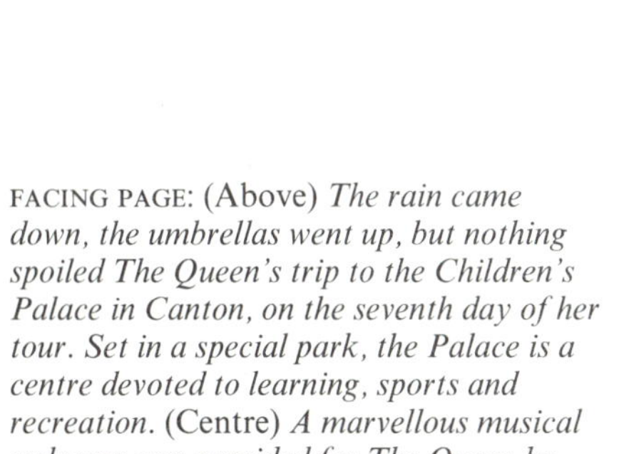

THIS PAGE: (Above) *The Queen returns the hospitality of President Li with a banquet on board* HMY Britannia, *ending the royal stay in Shanghai. The Queen and Prince Philip were photographed standing with President Li and his wife Madame Lin Jiamei.*

THIS PAGE: (Below) *The Queen is wearing an evening dress of aquamarine lace, with an aquamarine and diamond tiara, necklace and ear-rings.*

FACING PAGE: (Above) *Her Majesty's Yacht* Britannia *at anchor in Hong Kong harbour shortly after her arrival on 21 October.*

FACING PAGE: (Below) *A week earlier at the invitation of The Queen, a 'Sea Day' seminar on Sino-British trade was held on board whilst the Royal Yacht cruised off Shanghai. This picture shows the many Chinese and British businessmen who attended the seminar. In the centre in the light suit is Sir James Cleminson, Chairman of The British Overseas Trade Board; on his left is Li Zhaoji, Vice-Mayor of Shanghai; on his right is Mr Gordon Sloan, President of the 48 Group, and Sir Eric Sharp, President of the Sino-British Trade Council and Chairman of Cable and Wireless.*

To reach the Western Hills and these temples, The Queen and Prince Philip drove along part of the infamous 'Burma Road' which crossed the mountains from Burma to Kunming. In fact, Kunming's modern expansion can be dated from World War II when refugees from Japanese-occupied areas of China and Indo-China arrived in large numbers, and the airfield at Kunming was the end of the air supply line 'over the hump' of the Himalayas from India.

A midday trip by boat across Lake Dianchi brought The Queen to Daguan Park, first built in 1690. The park is hemmed in by a long dyke and is dotted with rainbow-shaped bridges, willow-tree groves, and lovely pavilions and terraces. It is also a year-round paradise of flowers, including two rose gardens—and here The Queen and Prince Philip planted a new English rose called 'Volunteer'. The bloom—yellow with a pinky tinge—is named after Voluntary Service Overseas workers, a group of whom, teaching English in Kunming, were presented to The Queen and Prince Philip. The rose is now on the market and part of the profits from sales will go to VSO.

The afternoon ended with a royal visit to the Kunming Institute for Nationalities. Approximately one-third of the 11 million population of Yunnan province belong to ethnic minorities; and 95 per cent of the Institute's 3000 students are from these minorities. The Institute has a museum with examples of traditional dress, jewellery, scripts and musical instruments.

In the evening—another banquet, hosted by the Governor of Yunnan, followed by a cultural performance.

*   *   *

FACING PAGE: (Above) *The Royal Party disembarking, appropriately, at Queen's Pier where they were received by the Governor of Hong Kong and Lady Youde. (Below left) The Queen, dressed in turquoise and white, inspecting the Guard of Honour. (Right, centre and below) A colourful 'Youth Spectacular' performance was held in The Queen's honour at the Hong Kong Coliseum.*

THIS PAGE: (Above) *A happy afternoon is spent at the Sha Tin racecourse, with its dramatic back-drop of skyscrapers and where more money passes through betting offices in one day than during the entire Royal Ascot Week.*

Day 7: Saturday 18 October

So, to the final stop on the fabulous 3000-mile royal tour of China—Canton, capital of Guangdong province, a city which for centuries was the traditional gateway of China. Again, as in Shanghai, the people flocked to the streets to give The Queen a tumultuous and smiling welcome. They lined the pavements 10–20 feet deep; they crowded windows and doorways. As I drove in the royal procession it seemed to me that all five-and-a-half million Cantonese had turned out to welcome The Queen as an old friend. And in a sense, they were, because it is here that the British trading connection with China first began over 200 years ago, Canton being the first Chinese city opened to foreigners. Historically the place has always been in the forefront of political and social change, and it remains one of China's busiest and most important links with the outside world. The vitality and energy of the city are shown in the bustling streets and shops. Roman traders are thought to have reached here in the second century AD; several hundred years later there was a flourishing Arab community; then came the first contact with Europeans when the Portuguese landed in Canton in 1514. The British

BRITISH AIRWAYS
EMERG
EXIT
HATS

did not arrive until 1625, some 60 years before the formal 'opening' of Canton in 1685. However, trade remained difficult for a long time after that, and for much of the 18th century foreigners were allowed to live in Canton for only seven months of the year. Even then they were restricted to Shamian Island, where there are still many old colonial-style buildings and, most impressively these days, The White Swan, a new international-standard luxury hotel opened in 1982. The hotel, which overlooks the Pearl River, takes its name from a Chinese legend, a white swan having carried away a folk hero, Huang Shaoyan, from Shamian, which means 'sandy flat'. It was here that European traders first established their factories, the island later becoming a British and French concession area.

After attending a luncheon given by the head of the government of Guangdong province in the White Swan Hotel, The Queen visited the Western Botanical Gardens and viewed the miniature landscapes. This traditional-style Chinese garden specialises in ornamental potted plants, and, in two exhibition areas and a courtyard, there are displays of more than 300 plants including miniature pine, fir, nandina, rattan, and elm trees. The oldest of the specimens is aged 150 years. The Queen planted an oak tree from Windsor Great Park and unveiled a commemorative plaque. Then she went on to a marvellous musical welcome by 300 children at the Canton Children's Palace. Built in 1952 in a specially-laid-out park, the Palace is a centre for learning, sports and recreation; with facilities for various activities which include reading, singing, painting, playing music, calligraphy, dancing, electronic games, biology, navigation, and astronomy. The children presented

★   ★   ★

FACING PAGE: (Above left) *The Queen and Prince Philip being shown round the Sha Tin racecourse by Sir Michael Sandberg, Chairman of the Royal Hong Kong Jockey Club, and Lady Sandberg.* (Above right) *Presenting a cup to a happy winner.*

FACING PAGE: (Below) *The Queen saying her farewells to the Governor of Hong Kong and Lady Youde, and waving goodbye from the doorway of the British Airways Tristar.*

THIS PAGE: (Above) *Prince Philip with Brigadier John Whitehead, Colonel of the Regiment, receiving garlands from a small boy.* (Below) *The Prince reviewing the 7th Duke of Edinburgh's Own Gurkha Rifles.*

the smiling Queen with a wooden model boat; then she visited specialist music and art classes before enjoying a children's concert and meeting some of the performers and teachers on stage. While The Queen was at the Children's Palace, The Duke of Edinburgh was fulfilling his separate and last engagement of the royal tour by visiting Huakeng village in the countryside near Canton. There he went into the rice paddy fields and had a look at cash crops including citrus fruit and bananas.

Finally—the royal departure. The Queen and Prince Philip boarded the Royal Yacht *Britannia*, which had docked at Huangpu New Port, 25 miles down the river from Canton, and held a farewell reception. The Royal Marines Beat the Retreat; then *Britannia* sailed off down the Pearl River while a terrific Chinese carnival was in full swing onshore. It was a fitting end to what The Queen, in her valedictory message to the Chinese leadership, described as an 'exhilarating' tour.

Days 8 and 9: Sunday 19 and Monday 20 October

With the Queen and Prince Philip on board, *Britannia* sailed in a leisurely way down the Pearl River and round the South China coast to Hong Kong. Her serene progress contrasted sharply with her earlier, tricky voyage south from Shanghai to Canton, when she was forced to battle against high seas and the threat of typhoon Ellen in order to ensure that the royal travel plans were not wrecked. *Britannia* reached her Canton berth two hours before schedule, despite what the British Naval Attaché called 'a good blow' ... so rough, in fact, that the Chinese pilot could not board her. *Britannia*, therefore, was guided up the Pearl River by a Chinese warship.

Days 10 to 12: Tuesday 21 to Thurday 23 October

The Queen was in Hong Kong again for the first time since 1975. Then, she had become the first reigning British monarch to visit the territory; now, she was witnessing a quite different Hong Kong. It is not just that the colony, with its five-and-a-half million inhabitants, has a million more people now than it did 11 years ago; and it is not just that the place has developed in an astonishingly vibrant way. What is really important is that the people of Hong Kong are trying, as realisitically as possible, to come to terms with their future—a future which lies with China rather than with Britain. As monarch, The Queen signed the Act agreeing to Chinese sovereignty over Hong Kong in 1997, another 11 years from now; and she referred to the Sino-British agreement in a speech she made at City Hall on her arrival. Her historic visit to China, she said, 'symbolised the new relationship between Britain and China, a relationship in which the agreement between the two countries on the future of Hong Kong has played a significant part'. She went on: 'You have been promised in that agreement that the institutions, traditions, and way of life so important to the people of Hong Kong will be preserved. The agreement, and the firm commitment by the Governments of the United Kingdom and China enshrined in it, will I trust, be an assurance and an encouragement to you as you face the challenges of the future.'

*   *   *

ABOVE: *After the review Prince Philip met some of the wives of the Gurkhas and as he drove away these magnificent soldiers surged around his car to wish him farewell.*

The Queen added that she was sure that Hong Kong's future development would continue to draw from both Chinese and British traditions. Because Hong Kong has been able to profit from these traditions, its people have rapidly adapted to progress where 'less adaptable folk might well have succumbed'. She concluded: 'As you move towards a new phase in your development our thoughts will always be with you.'

The speech followed immediately upon The Queen stepping ashore at Hong Kong after the spectacular arrival in Victoria Harbour of *Britannia* and her escort vessels. There was a fly-past, a 21-gun salute, bands played, ships' sirens hooted, and water jets cascaded from fire-boats. Other highlights of the visit included a happy afternoon for The Queen at the Royal Hong Kong Jockey Club, where, on any single day, more money is bet than for the whole of Royal Ascot Week in England. There was happiness, too, for one small Chinese boy, eight-year-old Ho-Lun Tung, known to his British friends as Alan, who shyly asked The Queen to sign his programme, and who was quite overwhelmed when she responded. The Queen does not normally give autographs, but on this occasion she made an exception and very kindly wrote: 'Elizabeth R., 1986'.

Prince Philip stayed behind in Hong Kong to review the Seventh Duke of Edinburgh's Own Gurkha Rifles, so the night before *Britannia* sailed The Queen and Prince Philip held a final dinner and reception on board the Royal Yacht; fireworks glittered over the harbour and, once again the Royal Marines Beat the Retreat, a ritual this time overlaid with a unique symbolism and significance as the people of China, Hong Kong and Britain together look to the future.